W9-BWT-190

BE AN HVAC TECHNICIAN

GUIDE TO THE TRADES

Published in the United States of America by Cherry Lake Publishing
Ann Arbor, Michigan
www.cherrylakepublishing.com

Content Adviser: Daniel Sanchez, Career and Technical Education Teacher, Prosser Career Academy, Chicago, IL
To my daughters, Margot Delia Arrington and Isla Leticia Gross, for being the igniter and fire that light papa's furnace everyday.
Reading Adviser: Marla Conn, MS, Ed., Literacy specialist, Read-Ability, Inc.

Photo Credits: Cover and page 1, ©rakratchada/Shutterstock; pages 5 and 20, ©fstop123/iStockphoto.com; pages 6, 11, 22, and 26, ©ALPA PROD/Shutterstock; page 8, ©Suwin/Shutterstock; page 12, ©Joyseulay/Shutterstock; page 14, ©Lisa F. Young/Shutterstock; page 17, ©urbans/Shutterstock; page 18, ©Andrey_Popov/Shutterstock; page 23, ©Magsi/Shutterstock; page 25, ©Geo Martinez/Shutterstock; page 28, ©David Spates/Shutterstock

Library of Congress Cataloging-in-Publication Data
Names: Mara, Wil, author.
Title: Be an HVAC technician / by Wil Mara.
Description: Ann Arbor, Michigan : Cherry Lake Publishing, [2019] | Series: 21st century skills library | Includes bibliographical references and index.
Identifiers: LCCN 2019003499| ISBN 9781534148208 (lib. bdg.) | ISBN 9781534149632 (pdf) | ISBN 9781534151062 (pbk.) | ISBN 9781534152496 (ebook)
Subjects: LCSH: Heating—Vocational guidance—Juvenile literature. | Air conditioning—Vocational guidance—Juvenile literature.
Classification: LCC TH7224 .M37 2019 | DDC 697.0023/73—dc23
LC record available at https://lccn.loc.gov/2019003499

Cherry Lake Publishing would like to acknowledge the work of The Partnership for 21st Century Learning.
Please visit *www.p21.org* for more information.

Printed in the United States of America
Corporate Graphics

ABOUT THE AUTHOR

Wil Mara is the author of over 175 fiction and nonfiction books for children. He has written many titles for Cherry Lake Publishing, including the popular *Global Citizens: Modern Media* and *Citizen's Guide* series. More about his work can be found at www.wilmara.com.

TABLE OF CONTENTS

Going to Work

It's early in the morning, and Dana Milner is in her truck on her way to a job **site**. She's an HVAC technician. HVAC stands for heating, **ventilation**, and air-conditioning. These are things that control the temperature and air quality inside a building. Dana has always been interested in HVAC work. Even as a kid, she thought it was really neat that her house could be warm in the winter and cool in the summer. And she thought it was even neater that she could have a career working with HVAC technologies and make a good living at it.

Now Dana is in her mid-thirties and running her own HVAC business. Sometimes she works independently, mainly

HVAC technicians help make sure that people's homes stay cool during hot weather and warm during cold weather.

in people's homes. If a customer's furnace stops working in the middle of the night, she'll go over and fix it. The problem might be a frozen line or a clogged filter. Or maybe the furnace's igniter went out, so the furnace can't even get started. Either way, Dana knows she'll be able to identify the problem and fix it. She likes the feeling of helping people. After all, there are few things worse than being without heat on a cold winter night!

Making sure that air flows through a building correctly is a big part of regulating the building's temperature.

Sometimes Dana works for a contractor. A contractor hires professionals to do various types of work on a building as it is being constructed. Some people work on the carpentry, others handle the plumbing, and Dana will help install the HVAC systems. Because she lives in an area that has both cold and warm seasons, she installs furnaces and air-conditioning units. She also installs ventilation systems. Ventilation allows fresh air to **circulate** through a structure while getting rid of stale air.

This day, Dana will be working for a contractor. She arrives at the job site at exactly 7:30 a.m. This gives her time to meet with the project's **foreman**, who acts as her boss during the course of this job. They go over the **blueprints** and discuss what needs to be done. Blueprints are technical documents that show the design of a new building down to the smallest detail. Dana finds these kinds of plans really interesting and has always enjoyed looking them over. Today, she sees that she'll be working in the basement, connecting ventilation

21st Century Content

There are about 333,000 HVAC technicians working in the United States today. The five states that employ the most HVAC techs are listed below, along with the most current employment numbers available.

- Florida—29,500
- California—25,000
- Texas—23,500
- New York—18,500
- Pennsylvania—14,000

An HVAC technician installs filters to help clean the air that flows through a building.

ducts to the building's heating system. For the last few days, she and her fellow workers have been setting up the heating system itself. This one runs on natural gas, which is highly flammable. The workers have been very careful to make sure that none of the system's pipes have even the tiniest leak.

Another HVAC technician shows up a few minutes after Dana. His name is Bobby, and he is Dana's **apprentice**. An apprentice is an HVAC tech who is in training under the watchful eye of a more experienced worker. Dana likes Bobby very much. He is a good listener and is very eager to learn. She also likes the fact that she is helping someone else start a career. Bobby's apprenticeship with Dana is in its third year. After one more year, Bobby can take the test to earn his certification to work on his own without supervision. Dana is sure he'll pass it. And that's good news, because he'll be joining a growing workforce. Job growth in the HVAC field is rising at a rate of about 15 percent each year. This is much higher than most other professions.

A food truck pulls up near the building site, and Dana and Bobby get some coffee and egg sandwiches. Then it's time to get to work. They go to Dana's truck and collect all the tools they'll need for the day, including a tape measure, a power drill, screwdrivers, pipe cutters, and sheet metal cutters. Then they go into the basement with the others. If all goes according to plan, the heating system will be ready for testing by the end of the day. And if there are no problems, they'll be able to start on the air-conditioning system the next day. Dana and Bobby both really like this part of their profession—the way each day can be a little different from the previous one, with new challenges to face all the time.

Learning the Ropes

Modern HVAC systems can be very complicated. Every building has different needs. Knowing how to **efficiently** control temperature, airflow, and **humidity** in different environments requires a great deal of specialized knowledge. This means HVAC technicians require a lot of education and training to be good at their jobs.

An HVAC tech's formal education starts in high school. High schools do not usually offer courses dealing with HVAC technologies. But the general subjects typically taught in high school are all important to future HVAC techs. For example, HVAC techs will use math skills to do things such as calculate the correct size for new ductwork. Physics, chemistry, and

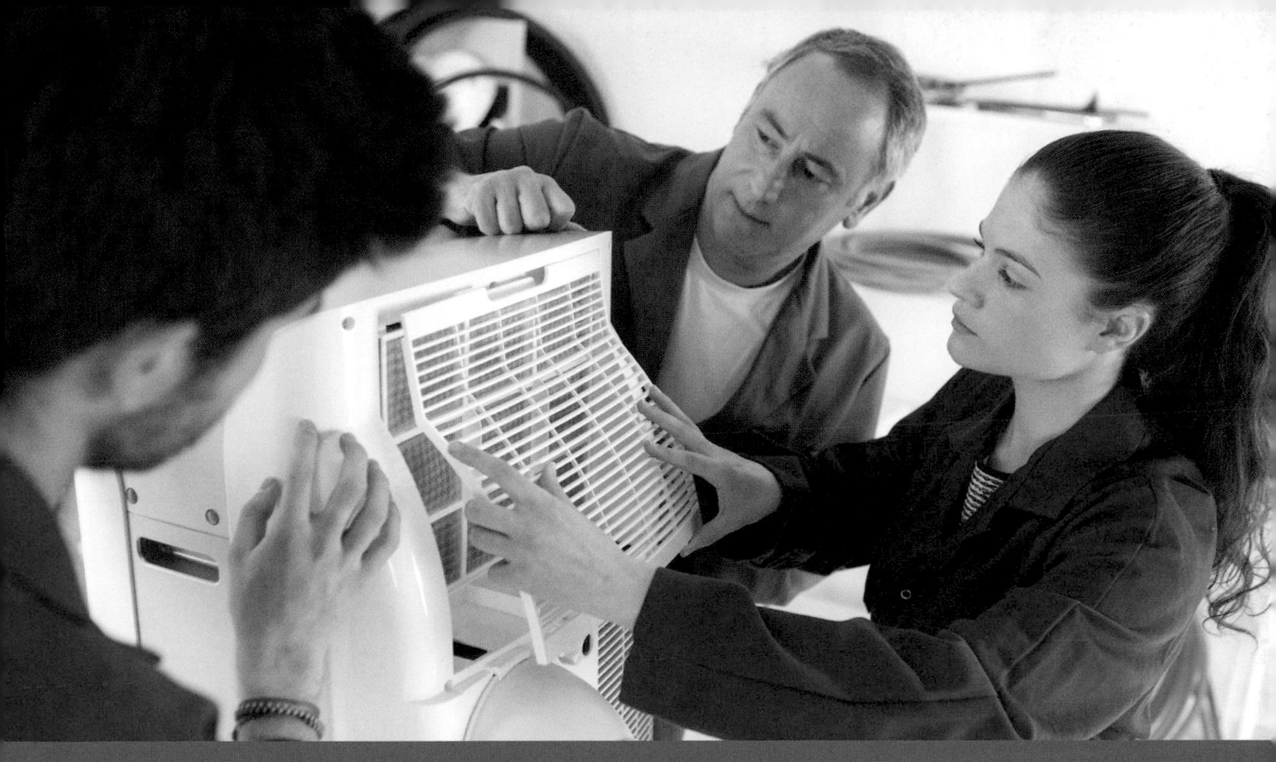

Hands-on learning is one of the best ways for a student to discover how different HVAC systems work.

other science subjects will help future HVAC techs understand the properties of heat energy and learn how air moves and changes under different conditions. And any kind of industrial trade class (sometimes called "shop class") will give students experience working with various tools.

After high school, students who wish to become HVAC techs generally enroll in a trade or vocational school or a community college. Such programs can last anywhere from six months to two years. During this time, students will begin

An HVAC technician uses gauges to measure the pressure of air flowing into and out of an air-conditioning unit.

to learn the ins and outs of the HVAC trade. They will take classes to study how HVAC systems are designed. They will learn how air moves through different kinds of ductwork and piping. They will find out how to determine how much power is needed to heat and cool spaces of different sizes and shapes. They will also study building **codes** and learn about safety regulations in the HVAC trade.

Reading, studying, and listening to lectures are all part of learning to become an HVAC tech. However, there is a lot more to an HVAC education than standard classroom studies. Students spend a lot of their time getting hands-on experience. They get to practice using the same tools they'll use when they're on the job someday. Common tools of the trade include everything from simple hammers and screwdrivers to power tools like drills and torches.

HVAC students also learn to take measurements and perform tests on HVAC equipment using a variety of specialized devices. Multimeters help them measure the strength of electrical currents. This is important because most HVAC systems rely at least partially on electricity. Pressure gauges help HVAC techs measure air, water, and gas pressure. Psychrometers are used to track airflow.

Safety is an important topic for all HVAC students. They will learn how to correctly use protective gear such as boots, gloves, helmets, safety glasses, and earmuffs or earplugs. They will also find out how to avoid potential accidents by taking the proper precautions.

After a future HVAC tech's schooling is complete, it is time to seek out an apprenticeship. During an apprenticeship, a

Mentors share their experienced knowledge of their trade with apprentices who still have much to learn.

student learns the HVAC trade while working with a professional technician in real job situations. This is a very important step in the learning process. It enables a student to make mistakes while practicing without any great cost to themselves or to customers. The **mentor** tech keeps a close eye on the student until he or she has enough experience to work alone. Apprenticeships can be a lot of fun for both the student and the mentor, particularly if they get along well.

An apprentice's ultimate goal is to become a certified

technician capable of working without supervision. The requirements to reach this point vary from state to state. For example, some states require an apprenticeship to last between three and five years. Others may measure their requirements down to precise hours, such as 2,000 hours of annual on-the-job training along with 150 hours of technical education. Either way, an apprentice who meets these requirements is ready to begin working as a professional.

Life and Career Skills

Some HVAC techs focus only on new installations. This means they are called in to install HVAC systems in new homes, offices, and other buildings under construction. These specialists are very good at reading and understanding blueprints and other plans. Many are able to design new HVAC systems themselves.

Other HVAC techs dedicate themselves to the repair and replacement of existing systems. These experts approach the job in an entirely different way. They start most projects by running a series of tests to detect and understand the problem with the existing system. Then they figure out the best way to fix it.

Hot and Cold

HVAC work can be tough at times, but in a very good way. An HVAC technician always has new challenges to overcome and problems to solve. There is very little chance of getting bored on the job!

The start of the average workday can vary depending on what type of work a tech is doing. Installing the air-conditioning or heating system during the construction of a new building will probably result in a fairly normal schedule. The tech might arrive at the job site around 8:00 a.m. and leave to go home around 4:30 p.m. This type of comfortable work schedule is common for techs who specialize in installing new systems.

Large buildings often have complex ventilation systems with huge ducts.

Techs who specialize in the repair of existing systems tend to have a much less predictable schedule. HVAC systems are expected to work pretty much all the time. So if a heating unit breaks down in the middle of the night in the dead of winter, it will need to be repaired right away. This means an HVAC tech might be awakened and have to climb out of a warm bed to go fix the problem. This isn't necessarily a bad thing, though. It can be very rewarding to help people out in tough situations. After all, everyone loves the person who

Customers are sure to be grateful to HVAC techs who arrive promptly to fix a broken air conditioner on a sweltering summer day.

can get their furnace working when it's below freezing outside!

The HVAC trade can require workers to be very social, but it doesn't require nonstop conversation. At different times, HVAC technicians get to work both alone and with people. Some jobs can be handled by a lone technician. Aside from discussing the problem with the customer, the tech can work alone in peace. But on a bigger job, a tech might be part of a team that works together all day long until a project is finished. This type of work requires plenty of cooperation and communication.

Anyone interested in the HVAC field can choose to specialize in the type of work that suits their personality best. Those who prefer to work by themselves will lean toward smaller jobs such as home repair. Those with outgoing personalities who enjoy the company of others will do well in more complicated jobs that stretch over the course of many weeks or months.

Life and Career Skills

Some HVAC technicians are generalists. This means they develop their skills and experience across all areas of the job. They are pretty good at everything, but they lack a specialty.

Others choose to specialize in one or two areas. One HVAC technician might deal almost entirely with air-conditioning systems. Another might be an expert in heating systems. There is also an area of the trade that deals specifically with refrigeration. For example, workers who specialize in this area might work with the powerful refrigeration units used to keep food cold in supermarkets or restaurants.

A positive, friendly attitude can help make any job go smoothly.

Certain personality traits can come in handy on the job. For example, it is very important for HVAC techs to be good with small details. Repair work is often a matter of conducting tests until the problem is found, then taking the system apart to replace or clean one tiny part. Patience is also very important for HVAC techs. There are times when the solution to a problem will not be easy to determine. Or a part in need of replacing might be difficult to reach. What seems like a simple job at first can sometimes end up taking a very long time.

HVAC techs should also try to stay in good physical shape. The job can be physically demanding. It's not unusual for a tech to spend long hours standing, crouching, or lying in tight spaces. They sometimes have to carry heavy gear and set heavy equipment into place. Working outside is common, even on days when the weather isn't particularly pleasant.

The pay for the average HVAC technician is somewhere around $47,000 per year, or roughly $22.50 per hour. However, experienced technicians often earn far more than this. There are also opportunities to work overtime hours. These are hours beyond the standard 40-hour workweek. During overtime, a tech's pay is generally increased to one-and-a-half or twice as much as usual. However, overtime is usually logged during weeknights, weekends, and sometimes even holidays. This means techs are trading their personal time for extra pay.

Many HVAC techs are **union** members. A labor union is an organization of workers who band together to negotiate for better pay and other benefits from employers. Union members often receive benefits such as a retirement plan or health insurance. Unions also protect members from mistreatment

HVAC emergencies can happen at any time of day, and some techs work odd hours to help out in these situations.

The chance to work outdoors on a sunny day from time to time is one of the many perks of working as an HVAC tech.

by employers and help members find work. In return, members pay dues to the union to fund its continued operation.

Rules and Regulations

In many parts of the world, HVAC systems are a necessity to keep people healthy and comfortable. If these systems do not work correctly during extreme weather, people can be left to endure dangerous temperatures. There are also many potential dangers associated with HVAC systems. They are connected to electrical and gas systems, which can cause fires or explosions if used incorrectly. For these and other reasons, there are many laws and regulations in place to oversee the use of HVAC technology.

Some of these regulations take the form of building codes. These are rules that HVAC technicians and other trade workers must follow when doing any kind of construction work. For example, codes might determine the ways that air can be vented

An HVAC tech uses a multimeter to check the flow of electricity in a thermostat.

out of a building. Or they might require techs to use specific kinds of materials when installing a new system. Building codes ensure that new construction projects are built safely. They also make sure that HVAC systems do not waste energy. Codes can vary from one location to another, and they can change over time. HVAC techs are required to stay up-to-date with the latest codes and standards.

Other regulations are designed to ensure that all HVAC technicians are properly educated and qualified to do a good

Customers can rest assured that a licensed and bonded HVAC technician is likely to do quality work.

job. The installation or maintenance of an air conditioner, a furnace, or other HVAC equipment is not a do-it-yourself project. It always requires the services of a technician who is both licensed and **bonded**.

A license is legal permission to work in a certain area. Most of the time, licenses are issued at the state level. Each state has its own licensing requirements. In some cases, licensing is issued at a lower level of government, such as the county or city. In most states, operating without a license is against the law and can result in all sorts of legal trouble.

The requirements for becoming a licensed HVAC technician can vary from place to place. However, they all require a certain amount of on-the-job experience. They

21st Century Content

HVAC technicians work in a variety of places. Some of the most common include homes, hospitals, factories, stores, offices, and schools. Most HVAC work is done indoors, although some outdoor work does occur from time to time. For example, while the ducts for an air-conditioning system will need to be installed on the inside, the air-conditioning units themselves will more than likely be set up outside. This is because an air-conditioning system is in fact transferring heat from your home to the outdoors.

Roughly two out of every three HVAC technicians work for contractors. About another 9 percent are self-employed. This means that while they may get occasional contract work, most of the time they are directly employed by their customers. Other HVAC techs are hired privately by companies or government organizations. These techs work as needed on the various buildings owned or operated by their employers.

Because some HVAC jobs require dangerous tools, there is always a chance for accidents. However, a good tech always uses safety gear to help prevent injuries.

might also require technicians to pass a test proving that they understand the safe, correct way to install and work on different kinds of HVAC systems.

In many cases, an HVAC tech must also secure what's known as a bond. A bond is a type of insurance policy. It covers any damage caused by an HVAC technician while working. It also covers the costs created by a job left unfinished.

An HVAC technician never intends to damage property or cause other problems for a customer. However, accidents can happen from time to time. A tool could malfunction. A technician could slip and make a mistake. In these kinds of situations, a bond will cover the costs of any damage. This prevents technicians or their employers from having to pay those costs.

In rare situations, technicians might be forced to leave a job unfinished. For example, they might get sick or an emergency could arise. And every now and then, a tech may work a job that turns out to have problems right from the start. In this case, a contractor would probably rather hire someone different instead of using the same HVAC technician to fix the problem. Again, the insurance provided by a bond will cover these expenses.

It is easier for some HVAC techs to obtain a bond than it is for others. Those who have a lot of work experience and few mistakes on their records will have no trouble finding an insurance company to work with. But those who have used their bonds before and cost the insurers through their mistakes will have a harder time getting new coverage. If a tech makes too many mistakes on the job, it might even become impossible to get another bond at all.

Think About It

Humans have been coming up with ways to stay warm in the cold and cool in the heat for a very long time. Ancient Romans heated their homes with devices called braziers. Braziers looked like steel cages and held wood for burning. The Romans also created systems that ran heated air beneath the flooring of their homes during the colder parts of the year. The ancient Egyptians developed a very early form of air-conditioning—they would hang wet reeds by open windows to cool the breezes as they blew inside. How well do you think these early attempts at heating and cooling worked compared to modern HVAC systems? Can you think of other ways to heat or cool a room without using a furnace or air conditioner?

There are many different paths one can take within the HVAC industry. Which one would you like best? Why? Explain your answer in as much detail as possible. What parts of the job do you think you'd like best?

Find Out More

BOOKS

Bickerstaff, Linda. *Careers in Heating, Ventilation, and Air Conditioning (HVAC).* New York: Rosen Classroom, 2013.

Masters, Nancy Robinson. *How Did That Get to My House? Electricity.* Ann Arbor, MI: Cherry Lake Publishing, 2010.

WEBSITES

HowStuffWorks—How Air Conditioners Work
https://home.howstuffworks.com/ac1.htm
Learn more about different kinds of air-conditioning systems and how they work.

U.S. Bureau of Labor Statistics—Occupational Outlook Handbook: Heating, Air Conditioning, and Refrigeration Mechanics and Installers
https://www.bls.gov/ooh/installation-maintenance-and-repair/heating-air-conditioning-and-refrigeration-mechanics-and-installers.htm
Learn how to become an HVAC technician and more about the profession at this government site.

GLOSSARY

apprentice (uh-PREN-tis) someone who is learning a skill by working with an expert on the job

blueprints (BLOO-printz) drawings that illustrate how a structure needs to be built

bonded (BAHND-id) having an insurance policy to cover damages caused by a worker while on the job

circulate (SUR-kyuh-late) to move in a circle or pattern, such as air through a ventilation system

codes (KOHDZ) rules that determine the correct design and installation of an HVAC system

ducts (DUKTS) tubes through which air or other gases move within a system

efficiently (ih-FISH-uhnt-lee) working well while wasting as few resources as possible

foreman (FOR-muhn) the person in charge of a construction job

humidity (hyoo-MID-ih-tee) a measurement of how much moisture is in the air

mentor (MEN-tor) someone who teaches a less experienced person

site (SITE) location of a job

union (YOON-yuhn) an organization that protects the interests of a certain type of worker, such as an HVAC technician

ventilation (ven-tuh-LAY-shuhn) process by which stale air is removed and fresh air is introduced into an environment

INDEX